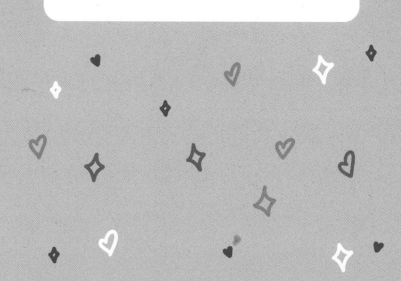

THIS BOOK BELONGS TO:

_____

Stormie Omartian

The Power of a Praying® Girl

HARVEST HOUSE PUBLISHERS
EUGENE, OREGON

Unless otherwise indicated, all Scripture quotations are taken from the New King James Version®. Copyright © 1982 by Thomas Nelson, Inc. Used by permission. All rights reserved.

Verses marked NIV are taken from the Holy Bible, New International Version®, NIV®. Copyright © 1973, 1978, 1984, 2011 by Biblica, Inc.® Used by permission. All rights reserved worldwide.

Cover design and hand lettering by Emily Weigel / Emily Weigel Design

Interior design by Janelle Coury

For bulk, special sales, or ministry purchases, please call 1-800-547-8979. Email: Customer service@hhpbooks.com

THE POWER OF A PRAYING is a federally registered trademark of The Hawkins Children's LLC. Harvest House Publishers, Inc., is the exclusive licensee of the federally registered trademark THE POWER OF A PRAYING.

is a federally registered trademark of the Hawkins Children's LLC. Harvest House Publishers, Inc., is the exclusive licensee of the trademark.

Italics in quoted Scriptures indicate emphasis added by the author.

THE POWER OF A PRAYING® GIRL

Copyright © 2021 by Stormie Omartian
Published by Harvest House Publishers
Eugene, Oregon 97408
www.harvesthousepublishers.com

ISBN 978-0-7369-8371-6 (pbk.)
ISBN 978-0-7369-8372-3 (eBook)

Printed in the United States of America

23 24 25 26 27 28 29 / VP / 10 9 8 7 6 5 4 3 2

Jesus said,
"Let the little children come to me,
and do not hinder them,
for the kingdom of God belongs to such as these."
Mark 10:14 NIV

With special thanks to my two
consultants, who are experts in this field:
London (age 8) and
Lola Rose (age 12)

You are godly girls with godly parents,
and you inspired me more
than I can adequately express.

Contents

1

Do My Prayers Matter to God?

Do you know that God is real and He loves you very much? Do you know you can talk to God whenever you want? He says your prayers are important to Him because He cares about what *you* care about. That's because He cares about *you*. It doesn't matter how *big* or *small* you are, or how *old* or *young* you are, or how *powerful* or *weak* you feel. God listens to you when you pray to Him.

Prayer is talking to God. You can tell God anything that is on your heart. But prayer is not telling God what to do. Prayer is sharing with God what you would *like* Him to do. He always wants to hear from you, so it's good to talk to God every day. Just know He will answer your prayers in *His* way and in *His* time. This book will help you talk to God, and it won't be hard. It will be easy. Soon, talking to God will be something you just naturally want to do. It's like sharing what is in your heart every day with your best friend.

Remember...

You can talk out loud to God. Or you can talk so softly to Him that only *He* can hear you. You can even pray to Him in your mind, and He will hear your thoughts.

When you first start talking to God, tell Him what you love about Him. Tell Him how much you appreciate all the things He has done for you and has given to you. That is called *praise*. Just like you talk to your family members and friends because you love them, you talk to God because you love Him too. God says if you love Him and live *His* way, you can call Him your friend.

WHAT THE BIBLE SAYS

Jesus said, "You are My friends
if you do whatever I command you."
John 15:14

Do you know you can pray to God anywhere you want to? That's because God always hears you no matter where you are. You can be outside or inside. You can be lying down quietly in your room, or walking outside where it's noisy and busy. Or you can be kneeling in a quiet place like Jesus did when He prayed. Where do *you* most like to talk to God? (Answer in pencil.)

_____

_____

WHAT OTHER GIRLS SAY...

Some of the *places* girls like to pray:
"In the shower or bathtub."
"In the car or wherever I'm walking."
"On my way to school."
"In church."
"Wherever I can be by myself."
"In my bed at night."
"Wherever I am."

You can talk to God whenever you want to. Just call His name. The Bible says if you draw near to God, He will draw near to you (James 4:8). When you say, "Dear Lord," or "I love You, God," or "Help me, Lord," that means you are wanting to be near Him and talk to Him. When He knows you want to get closer to Him, He comes closer to you. And He will hear you any time of day or night. You can be any place in the world—even on a boat in the middle of the ocean, or alone in a forest or a desert. Because He loves you, He is never too busy to hear your prayers.

Remember...

It doesn't matter *when* or *where* you talk to God.
He's always waiting to hear from you.

Jesus is God's Son. His mother, Mary, was pure and kind, and she loved God so much that He chose her to be the mother of Jesus. God revealed to people that His Son would be born on earth, and He would grow up to teach all who believe in Him how to live in a way that pleases God. When Jesus grew up, He told people He was the Son of God and they needed to receive Him as their Savior.

He said He would lay down His life for them so they could be saved from the consequences of their sins. *Sins* are anything we do that God doesn't like and are against God's laws and ways. *Consequences* are the bad things that happen when we do something wrong. God has laws for *our* benefit. He wants *us* to live *His* way because that's the way our lives work best. And if we reject evil and invite God's Son, Jesus, into our heart, we can live forever with Him in His heavenly Father's kingdom. I've read that heaven is a spectacular place, and you don't want to miss it. But if you have already received Jesus, you won't have to worry about that.

God loves children of all ages. But no matter how old you become, you will still be God's child. When Jesus went about preaching to people, He always welcomed the children who came to see Him, and He asked His disciples to never keep them away from Him. In fact, Jesus wanted adult people to receive Him too, but He told them they needed to come to Him just like a child would. A child has a heart of *love* and *trust*, and is very *humble*. Having a humble heart means you believe God is greater than anyone else, including yourself. God says to adults that they had better start acting like children if they want Him to listen to their prayers.

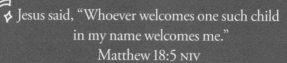

WHAT THE BIBLE SAYS

Jesus said, "Whoever welcomes one such child
in my name welcomes me."
Matthew 18:5 NIV

If you have invited Jesus to live in your heart, then you belong to Him. That means His Spirit lives inside you. If you have never received Jesus in your heart, you can do that right now. Just say the following words to Jesus:

> Lord Jesus, I invite You to come into my heart. I believe You are God's Son and You gave Your life on earth for me so that I can have life with You—both now and forever. Please forgive me for anything I have done wrong. Help me to always live Your way.

Write down your name: _____

Write down the date you said this prayer: _____

Write down the age you were when you said this prayer: _____

If you have already received Jesus, write down in the spaces above what day and year that was, and how old you were. It's always good to at least know the approximate date you received the Lord so you can look back and know that you did.

Jesus always respected children. He told adults they should never look down on children because *their angels* always see the *face* of *God* (Matthew 18:10). That means you always have at least one guardian angel watching over you, and that angel always sees God's face. That means your guardian angel has a direct connection with God. That also means you are very important to God because you are His child.

Here is some more good news about you and God. Because you are God's child, and He is the King of the universe, that means *you* are a *daughter of a king*. A king's daughter is always called a princess. That makes *you* a *princess*.

Remember...

Because you are a daughter of the
King of the universe, that makes *you*
GOD'S PRINCESS.

Jesus wants us all to pray in His name. That means when you talk to God and say, "In Jesus' name I pray" at the end of your prayer, it's like saying to God, "I know Your Son, and He is a personal friend of mine." And it's like God saying, "If you know My Son, then tell me what you want Me to do for you, because I want to do it." Every time you say, "In Jesus' name I pray," your prayers are made more powerful.

WHAT THE BIBLE SAYS

Jesus said, "If you ask anything in My name,
I will do it."
John 14:14

The Bible is also called God's Word. It helps you to learn about God, and what He *has done,* and what He *will do.* It tells you how much God loves you and what He wants to do in your life. It will also teach you how to think and live and pray in a way that makes God smile. It tells you about Jesus and all that He did for us. Reading God's Word will help you to know God better and talk to Him more. It pleases God. And pleasing God brings great *blessings* to you.

Blessings are the good things that happen in your life. If you have food to eat and a place to live and people who are kind to you, and love you, and take care of you, those are some of God's great blessings. Reading the Bible will always bring great blessings to you.

God is...

always waiting for you to talk to Him.

Praying is *communicating with God.* To communicate means to tell God your thoughts and feelings by talking, writing, or singing to Him. He loves for you to communicate with Him. And He wants to communicate with you too. People don't usually hear God's voice because *His Spirit* communicates with *their spirit.* But some people have. Most people hear God speaking to them in different ways. You might sense God speaking to your heart when you read His Word. Or when you pray and ask God to guide you, you might get a feeling in your heart that you are supposed to go a certain way and not another. Or He might give you an idea about what you *should* do, or *not* do, in a certain situation. Or He might remind you of something you need to do that you had forgotten until He reminded you.

In order to hear God speaking to your heart, you can't do all the talking without asking Him to show you something specific. You can say, "Lord, show me what to do about this person who is bothering me." Or, "Lord, show me how to stay safe today." Or, "Teach me how I can be a blessing to someone today." And He will bring things to your mind to help guide you.

♦ A QUESTION FOR YOU ♥

Even though you may be small, when you pray, big things can happen. What big thing do you want to pray about and see happen in your life or in someone else's life?

_____

_____

The Bible says God wants you to "pray without ceasing" (1 Thessalonians 5:17). That means God wants you to pray often about everything, and pray whenever you want to. This book will help you to pray like that. And it will remind you to pray about things you might forget. Read on to find important *things* and *people* for you to pray about, so you can have the blessed life God wants you to have.

My Prayer to God

Dear God, thank You that You are the King of the world and the universe, and also my heavenly Father. That means I am Your princess, and You have a good future for me. Help me to become all You created me to be. I love You, and I want to live Your way. Show me how to do that. Help me to talk to You every day. Teach me to read and understand Your Word—the Bible. Help me to remember that I am Your daughter so I will always act like it. In Jesus' name I pray.

Other things I want to remember to pray about are...

_____

_____

_____

_____

_____

_____

_____

_____

_____

_____

_____

2

Why Do I Sometimes Feel the Way I Do?

Do you ever have days when you feel down or anxious about something, and sometimes you are not even sure why?

Do you ever feel good one day, and the next day you wish you could just crawl into bed and pull the covers over your head?

We all have good days and not so good days. As a young girl, you especially can be having a good day in the morning, and then in the afternoon have a day filled with emotions that don't feel good and you don't know what just happened. This is not unusual at your age. And the reason for that is you are growing so fast, and in many different ways—mentally, emotionally, and physically.

It's easy to understand that you are *growing mentally* because you are studying and learning new things every day. And you can see that you are *growing physically* because you grow out of your clothes, and people keep telling you how grown up you're becoming. But it's not as easy to understand the ways you are *changing emotionally.*

Emotions are the way you feel. You can have *good feelings.* For example, you can feel happy, excited, loving, hopeful, cheerful, or peaceful. You can feel like you are having a good day, as if something good is going to happen. Those are *positive emotions,* and they make you feel happy and energetic. On the other hand, you can have feelings that make you *feel bad* and can *take away your energy* and cause you to feel tired, like you don't feel good enough to do what you need to do. For example, you can feel angry, insecure, nervous, lonely, or embarrassed—those are *negative feelings.* And some days you may feel them all within one day. Or you may feel very sad or stressed one day, and fine the next. You may have many different emotions, or perhaps you have one strong emotion that seems like it is trying to control your mind. Those emotions or feelings are especially uncomfortable if you don't understand why you are feeling that way.

Some days it's easy to figure out why you feel the way you are feeling, because you can look back at something that happened and know that made you feel bad. But when you cannot understand why you are feeling the way you do, you can ask God to show you. When you talk to God about it, He may show you some things you need to know. Or He may just take those negative feelings away and give you peace instead. Just thinking about how much God loves you can make a big difference in how you feel. When God shows you something, write it down. Also talk to your mom or dad, or a trusted family member, or a good, godly friend about it. Sometimes just talking about how you feel can cause those negative feelings to go away.

♪ A QUESTION FOR YOU ♥

Have you ever felt a negative emotion—like sadness, anger, hopelessness, worry, or fear—and you can't seem to get rid of that feeling? Do you feel that way now? Write down what you are feeling—or sometimes feel—and ask God to show you *what* it is exactly you are feeling, and *why* you feel that way. Complete this sentence. "Dear Lord, the way I sometimes feel is…"

_____

_____

_____

Do other people ever make you feel bad? Is it what they *say* or what they *do* that makes you feel bad? Or both? Is there anyone you can talk to or pray with about this? It's important that someone else knows what happened. Don't try to carry this burden alone. Write out a prayer below telling God who or what has made you feel bad. Ask Him to heal those hurt feelings and take them away.

_____

_____

_____

Remember...

People can be cruel,
but God is always kind and good.
You can ask God to help you find friends
who are kind and good like He is.

Your feelings don't have to control your life. It's important to see if you can figure out *why* you feel the way you do—if possible— because that will help you to try and do something to take care of the problem. But it's important to know that your feelings can change, and *you* can learn how to change them. Your negative feelings can become a habit without you even realizing it. So you have to start thinking like God's princess. A princess is important, kind, polite, smart, beautiful, and loved. You don't have to work hard to be that way. You just have to realize that's the way God made you.

If someone—like a bully or a rude and selfish person—is

mean to you and hurts your feelings, tell God and your mom or dad, or whoever takes care of you, or someone you trust who can pray with you. Ask God to take those hurtful words or actions that are in your memory and replace them with His love, and also ask Him to help you remember who He made you to be. Don't let those bad feelings play over and over in your mind. Those bad feelings aren't who you are. You are royalty because your heavenly Father God is the King. Because of who He made you to be, you have a great purpose. God is calling you to do great things.

Just know that you have control over your feelings. Maybe not at first when you find yourself feeling a certain way. But keep in mind that it is good to cry when your feelings hurt. Your tears can help to clean your mind and heart of bad feelings, so cry when you need to or want to. But remember that while you *don't have control* over what someone says or does, or over many things that happen in your life, you *do have control* over how it continues to affect you. You can go to God and say, "Dear Father God, please take away these sad feelings. Fill my heart and mind with Your love, peace, and joy, and push away the dark clouds over me so that Your light shines through."

Do you know you can have both negative and positive feelings at the same time? Often it helps to sort through the good and bad feelings you have and list them on opposite sides of a piece of paper, even if you just list one *negative* emotion and one *positive* emotion on each side. The point is, don't ignore your feelings. Bring them to God and tell Him how you feel. Ask God to help you think about the positive and not the negative. You can do this. Then list the good things about God and thank

Him for those things. Thank Him for the happy and positive feelings you have because of Him.

WHAT THE BIBLE SAYS

"Be *anxious* for *nothing*, but in *everything* by *prayer* and *supplication*, with *thanksgiving*, let your requests be made *known* to God; and the *peace* of God, which *surpasses* all understanding, will *guard* your *hearts* and *minds* through Christ Jesus."
Philippians 4:6-7

That means you are *not* supposed to be *anxious* about *anything*. Instead, you are to *pray* about *everything* and give thanks to God. When you do that, God will give you such peace that it will protect your heart and your mind. Isn't that a great promise from the Lord?

good all the time, and He loves you no matter what happens.

God says we don't have to suffer with bad days, because if we invite Him to take charge of *every day*, He will bring *good* in each day. That is why it's important to put God in charge every morning at the *beginning* of your day—or at the earliest time you remember to do it. Say, "Lord, be in charge of my life today. This is a day that You have made, and I will be glad about it because everything You do is good."

My Prayer to God

Dear Lord, I pray that You will always show me why I sometimes feel the way I do. Make it clear to me so I can understand. When I bring my negative feelings to You that I am struggling with, I pray You will lift me above them so they cannot bring me down. Thank You that You love me and care about the way I feel. Thank You that You hear my prayers, and I always receive good things from You. Thank You that You have instructed me in Your Word to "be anxious for nothing," but instead I should pray, and give thanks to You, and tell You about how I am feeling, and You will give me peace. Help me to bring everything that makes me worried and anxious to You. Thank You for the peace You pour into my heart that will guard my heart and mind from anything that is negative. In Jesus' name I pray.

Other things I want to remember to pray about are…

_____

_____

_____

_____

_____

_____

_____

_____

3

How Can I Always Be Myself?

*D*o you ever feel as if you have trouble being yourself? Does it sometimes seem like you don't know who "yourself" really is?

These feelings can happen when you are around people who make you feel uncomfortable, like you are not enough—not good enough, not smart enough, not dressed well enough, not talented enough, or whatever else they seem to suggest to you. But the way you *feel* around others is *not* who you *are*. You may have other times with certain people when you feel *comfortable*—like you *can* really be *yourself* because they understand and accept you the way you are.

Sometimes, however, those feelings come from *inside you* and reflect what you have been *thinking* about *yourself*. So it's not really other people's fault at all. That happens when the enemy of your soul lies to you about who God made you to be. And you believe those lies because you think they are the truth about you.

Let me explain something really important that you must know. That is, God has an enemy. This enemy was once a beautiful being God created to lead worship in heaven. His name was Lucifer, and he wanted to *be God*, so he led a third of the angels in heaven to follow him and rebel against God. But, of course, God is far stronger than anyone or anything, so He threw Lucifer and the rebellious angels out of heaven and they fell to earth. Now Lucifer is called Satan and his angels are demons, and they are all still rebelling against God as they try to lure everyone here to their side and rebel against God too.

You can't see these spiritual beings—just like can't see your *guardian angels* here on earth either. Guardian angels are the good angels who protect you.

God does not want you praying to angels. He wants you praying to *Him*. *He* is *God* of *all*, and no one else can even begin to answer your prayers. Only *He* can. But you don't have to worry about these evil beings because you have received Jesus in your heart. Even though evil beings see you as their enemy—and they will try to steal from you or lie to you in some way—they cannot touch you because you have the light of the Lord in you and you are God's. Your Father God loves and protects you. In fact, the better you know your heavenly Father, the better you understand that He is the King of the universe and you are His child. You are His princess. And that is final.

It's hard to know yourself really well right now because you are still learning about yourself and who God made you to be. You haven't lived with yourself long enough to know exactly how you feel about everything. You don't know each thing that makes you happy or sad, confident or insecure, excited or disinterested, hopeful or hopeless, grateful or angry. That's why writing down the things you *do* know about *you* is always helpful.

Just because you feel one way today doesn't mean you will feel that exact same way tomorrow, next week, or next year. But the more you write down how you feel and what you *do* know about yourself, the more you will grow to understand who you are. And that will help you to feel like yourself. So start with what you *do* know, and that is you are the daughter of a King and that makes you a part of a royal family. You are loved. You have worth and value, you have a purpose, and you have gifts and talents—and God has given you great power when you speak His Word or pray in Jesus' name. It doesn't matter if other people see all that yet. *God does!*

💙 A QUESTION FOR YOU 💙

How would you describe yourself? Are you loud, quiet, happy, sad, kind, friendly? What things do you enjoy doing? What things do you not like doing?

If there is not enough room to write down your answers here, get a notebook or a journal to write down your thoughts. Write them in pencil in case they change. That will be a helpful part of your getting to know yourself better.

_____

_____

_____

The more time you spend with God, the better you will know yourself, and the easier it will be when you are with others.

Remember...

The more you know who God is,
the more you will understand who you are.

A good friend is always someone you feel you can be your-self with. You are comfortable being *you* with her because you feel you can be completely honest about who you are. You can tell her about things you like and don't like. You can share with that person what is really bothering you. If you are often around a person who makes you feel bad about yourself, then there will soon come a day when you don't want to be around that person anymore. You will think of ways to avoid her. You will pray for a new friend who doesn't make you feel bad.

Talk to God every time you don't feel like yourself. Ask Him to show you why and what you can do to change that. Also, ask Him to help you know *Him* better. That always helps. The way to know Him better is by reading His Word and talking to Him in prayer every day. Tell Him how you feel, and thank Him for creating you to be a person who has the ability to make other people feel like themselves around *you*.

❦ WHAT OTHER GIRLS SAY... ❦

Some of the words girls use to describe themselves are:

"Helpful."   "Thankful."
"Kind."   "Fearful."
"Nervous."   "Worried."
"Caring."   "Loving."
"Happy."   "Friendly."

🖤 A QUESTION FOR YOU 🖤

What are several words you would use to *describe yourself*? You can use some of those listed above, or you can put down your own words.

_____

_____

_____

What are some words you would like *others* to *think* or *say* about *you*? (For example, "I would like people to think or say that I am friendly and kind.")

_____

_____

_____

Remember...

Getting to know who God made you
to be helps you to accept yourself better.
That takes time as you grow up.

WHAT THE BIBLE SAYS

"Do to others as you would have them do to you."
Luke 6:31 NIV

That means treating others the way you would like to be
treated, which is in a kind and thoughtful way. And it helps you
to stop focusing on yourself and start focusing on another person. That always makes you feel like yourself because you are a
kind person.

Don't let other people define you. That means don't let other
people decide who you really are. That is for you and God to
decide. And your parents too. They have your best interests at
heart as well. They want the best for you, and that's why they
work so hard.

Don't compare yourself to others. You are unique. That means
there is no other person in the world who is like you. You are

beautiful and wise because God gives you wisdom and beauty. He is beautiful. *His beauty in you* makes you *beautiful*. The Bible says of God that "He has made everything beautiful in its time" (Ecclesiastes 3:11). That means the beauty in a person takes time to develop. It doesn't depend on how you feel. You have to trust God's timing on everything.

Remember...

The more you understand
who your Father God is,
the more you will understand
who He made you to be.

Part of knowing yourself is being your own best friend. That means don't reject yourself. Don't criticize yourself. Appreciate who God made you to be. Ask God to show you the good things about yourself that you are not seeing. Learn what God thinks about you. The things you like and don't like about yourself can change in an instant as you grow up. Just because you are feeling sad one day does not make you a sad person. Say to yourself, "I am not an angry person. I am just *feeling* angry right now." *Be kind to yourself, not judging or criticizing yourself.* The more you *know yourself*, the more you will understand how to *be yourself*.

WHAT THE BIBLE SAYS

"I know the thoughts that
I think toward you, says the LORD,
thoughts of peace and not of evil,
to give you a future and a hope."
Jeremiah 29:11

That means God sees you in the great future He has for you. He sees you as *a person who is respected, who has* great worth because you are His daughter. Ask God to help you *see yourself* that way too. That doesn't mean you will think you are better than anyone else. It means that you love God and you respect how *He* thinks.

God is...

always accepting of you.

When God looks at you, He sees all the great things He has put in you. You may not see all those yet because they are still developing. Just because some other people might not see what God sees in you—yet—doesn't mean those qualities are not there.

God always accepts you the way you are, but He is not going to let you stay that way. That's why He is growing you up, and He will always want you to become more like Him. The more you become like Jesus, the more you will feel like yourself. And that will always be true.

My Prayer to God

Lord, help me to know You better so I can know myself better too. I want to be like You because You are kind and good and loving. Help me to have Your joy, patience, love, and goodness. Teach me to have the kind of character You have. Help me to *learn* more about You in Your Word so I can *become* more like You in my life. Show me how to be the best me I can be. Help me to focus on what I *can do*, and not what I feel I *can't do* right now. Keep me from comparing myself with others and instead help me to value everyone as unique, including myself. When I am tempted to have negative thoughts about myself, help me to turn to You and thank You for all the great things You see in me. In Jesus' name I pray.

Other things I want to remember to pray about are…

_____

_____

_____

_____

_____

_____

_____

_____

4

What Should I Do When I Feel Too Busy?

Do you ever feel like you are not doing anything well enough because you don't have enough time to do it all? Are you feeling pressure because of so many expectations of you that it seems like you can't ever live up to them? Many girls I have talked to say they feel too busy and their life seems out of control because of that.

It's because of the times we live in. We can see or know what everyone is doing all the time. And through what we see on television, computers, or in magazines, we may imagine this is a standard we must live up to. Girls like you are sometimes made to feel you have to be perfect every day. That is not how God wants you to feel at all. It's not good to always feel that way.

Feeling rushed all the time can cause stress in your mind, body, and emotions. Everyone needs time to just *be,* without having to think about all that you have to do every moment of every day. Girls, especially, need time to process their feelings and talk to God about all the things they are experiencing. If you are constantly *doing* and never having time to just *be*, then take time every day to *be* with the Lord. Or *be* with a family member just talking or doing something enjoyable together. Or just *be* with a book, reading it because *you* want to and not always as fast as you can because you have to.

God is...

everything I need.

Many girls have so many activities that they feel pressured because they want to be the best they can be in everything they do. The Bible does say it's not good to *never* be busy because then we can become lazy and don't do our work. Or we might spend time doing *unprofitable things*. That means doing things that don't matter and don't make you a better person. In fact, the Bible warns us about spending time with people who don't do much of anything. But to be so busy that you are stressed, with no time to just sit and talk to God and ask Him questions, and to be able to take time to catch up on your thoughts…that is not good. When you feel like that, God wants you to come near to Him so He can come near to you and give you His peace.

God wants us to do good things—things that are good for *us* and also good for *others*. But He doesn't want you to feel stressed about it, like you never really have enough time to live your life. God has given you the same amount of time every day as He has given everyone else. You don't have full control over your time because you are young, but you can ask God to help you make good use of your time. In other words, ask God to give you wisdom concerning how you use your time.

What are the things you need to do in any week? For example, go to school, practice a sport, study for a test, practice the piano, do homework, straighten up your room (or your bed, or your closet, or your things) or whatever you need to do to help your mom, or dad, or whoever takes care of you.

_____

_____

Write out a prayer asking God to show you how you could have more time to do those things better. For example, "Dear Lord, I would like to have more time to…"

_____

_____

_____

Ask your mom or dad, or whoever is taking care of you right now, to help you find 30 to 45 more minutes in your day just to have time to rest, or spend time with God being peaceful, or do something you really want to do but don't seem to ever have enough time to do it.

Remember...

It's okay to ask for help whenever you need it,
or to ask for some time off from your busy schedule,
rather than become frustrated and feel
like you can't handle your life.

Do you ever feel overwhelmed by all that you have to do? Do you sometimes feel like a failure because you don't have enough time to do things as well as you know you can?

♡ A QUESTION FOR YOU ♥

When that happens, what would make you feel better? Do you like to go outside to walk, or run, or jump, or ride your bicycle? Do you like to stay indoors and dance and be active? Do you have a pet that you like to play with? Do you like to lie on your bed and read a book? Do you like to color, draw, or paint?

_____

_____

_____

Is there any way you can schedule 30 to 45 minutes to do one of those things in a day? How could you do that?

_____

_____

_____

❦ WHAT OTHER GIRLS SAY... ❦

Some things girls like to do when they are stressed about feeling too busy:

"Listen to music."

"Paint, draw, or color."

"Do some physical activity."

"Sing a song I like."

"Dance to music."

"Play with my pet."

"Eat a snack."

"Talk to a friend or family member."

"Go outside."

When your schedule and your emotions make you feel overwhelmed, like your life is more than you can handle and you feel like you could explode, stop what you are doing as soon as you can and ask God for help. Tell Him you want Him to be in control of your life and your schedule.

WHAT THE BIBLE SAYS

"Trust in the LORD with all your heart,
and lean not on your own understanding;
in all your ways acknowledge Him,
and He shall direct your paths."
Proverbs 3:5-6

That means you need to trust God for everything, and not think you can figure it all out by yourself. You still need His help even when you decide how much you can do in a day. Ask God to show you how you can fit everything in that you must do. Ask Him if there is anything you can stop doing—or not spend as much time on—so you can do other things better. You have to do schoolwork, and you have to do the chores your parents ask you to do. They work very hard for you to have a home and good food and the things you need. They need your help. When you help them, God says He will bless you for that. And He will.

My Prayer to God

Dear Lord, sometimes I feel too busy and always in a hurry. I know You have given me a time for everything. If I have been putting too many expectations on myself, or I am trying too hard to do too much, show me the truth about that. Help me to lean on You, Lord. If other people are putting too many expectations on me—or at least more than I feel I have time to handle right now—help me to talk to my mother or father, or whoever is taking care of me, about that. Give that person an open heart to hear what I need to tell them. Thank You that You give me a time for everything in its season. Help me to see if I have tried to squeeze too many things into the same season. Teach me to understand how I can better use my time. Help me to take frequent moments to spend with You, soaking in Your peace. In Jesus' name I pray.

Other things I want to remember to pray about are…

_____

_____

_____

_____

_____

_____

_____

5

Does God Have a Purpose for My Life?

Do you realize that God has a great plan and a high purpose for your life? You don't have to know exactly what that is right now. You just have to know God has put gifts and talents in you that He will develop and use for good.

You may not be able to see your gifts and talents yet, but that doesn't mean God is not developing them at this very moment. Other people may be able to see them better than you can. Or perhaps *you* see them better than other people do. It doesn't matter who sees them. The most important thing is that *God* sees what He has put in you, and how He will use that for His glory and to bless others.

From the time I could hold a pencil and write words, I wanted to write all the time. I started when I was in first grade, creating stories and poems and songs out of the words I knew. I did not think about how successful I could be at writing, or how much money I could make, or how well known I could become. I thought only of how I loved to write. I would rather write than do anything else. I loved how words came alive and communicated to people. Words written well could cause people to see and feel things. But the important thing to me was when I wrote I felt free and peaceful. I felt energetic and happy. When I couldn't write, I was frustrated and not happy. I couldn't *not* write. I had to do it. I still feel that way today.

Even though I always had a sense that I wanted to be a writer, I still had no idea what to do about it. I did not know the Lord at all, so I had no idea that the Lord had a great purpose for my life and He could give me direction. And, of course, I didn't know how to pray to Him about anything. Once I received the Lord as my Savior and learned to pray to Him and seek Him for guidance about everything, He began to show me that doors for writing would open one by one. And they did.

It's good to see in yourself something you love to do so much that you want to do it every day. But you don't have to decide that right now. What is important now is to understand that you have value and purpose. A girl who never sees that she has a great purpose can waste her life either not preparing for the great things God has for her to do, or she may try to be like someone else she admires and not pursue who God made *her* to be. It's important for you to see that you will be happiest doing something you love. And you will always want to do it well. That could be anything from being a wife and a mother—which are two of the greatest callings in the world, and so much fun—to running a company, being a nurse or doctor, buying or selling, teaching, taking care of animals, or helping others in any way God shows you. It could be different things in different times of your life. It will be exciting to see what God has for you.

It's important that you realize you were created for greatness. That means God wants to do great things through you. You don't have to *make* it happen. You just have to follow God and *invite Him* to make it happen—*in you* and *for you*. The problem with *not* understanding that You are God's princess who is going to touch the lives of other people in a way that pleases God is that you can easily make poor choices in your life. But doing what *God wants* you to do will not only fulfill *your own purpose*, but also inspire *others* to find *their purpose* as well.

Remember...

You will always do well
the things you love doing most.

Every day you are growing into the princess God made you to be. All of your gifts and talents will take years to develop fully, but start asking God now to show you how He will use you to fulfill His purposes. You won't learn everything at once. It will take time to reveal the qualities He has put in you. But that doesn't mean you want to waste time on things that don't matter as you develop into the beautiful and important young woman He has created you to be. You don't want to settle for less than God has for you. Always ask God to show you what is good for you to do, and what is not so good.

Do you ever get compliments on something you do? It doesn't matter what it is—even if it seems like something that is not that important to you. For example, you may be surprised to learn how important it is to be a *kind* person, or an *understanding* person, or have the ability to *organize* something, or be good with children, or to *make* something, or *teach* another person, or be naturally *friendly,* or be an *encourager,* or a good talker, or be able to help people learn how to do something. Everything you do—even if it seems small to you—can be used in a big way to glorify God. Write down the things you can do that you or other people have noticed.

_____

_____

_____

Even if other people don't yet see it or say anything about it, what is something you *love* to do that you believe pleases God and blesses others? Write it down here even if you can't see how God could use that ability for His purpose in your life. God sees the potential in you that He put there.

_____

_____

_____

What do you *most love* to do? What would you want to do even if no one ever paid you to do it?

_____

_____

_____

❖ WHAT OTHER GIRLS SAY... ❖

What girls love to do most:
"Take care of pets."
"Sing or play music."
"Read or write."
"Help people."
"Take care of people who are sick."
"Teach people to do things."
"Draw, design, or paint things."
"Cook or prepare food."
"Fix things that are broken."
"Work with numbers."
"Tell people about God."

What are one or two things you find *easier* to do, or *more enjoyable* to do, than other things? Write them down even if you don't think they are very important. You may be surprised how much someone would appreciate your ability to do one of these things if you were doing it for them. (You can choose from the list on page 49 if you want.)

_____

_____

_____

WHAT THE BIBLE SAYS

"Humble yourselves
under the mighty hand of God,
that He may exalt you in due time,
casting all your care upon Him, for He cares for you."
1 Peter 5:6-7

This means you should thank God for the gifts, abilities, and talents He has put in you, and trust that at the right time He will cause others to recognize and appreciate them too. You don't have to worry about when or how this will happen. You just have to give your concerns to God when you pray, knowing that He cares about you and always has you in His mind. If you are humble before God, He will lift you up and reveal your gifts and talents when the time is right and you are ready.

WHAT THE BIBLE SAYS

"May He grant you
according to your heart's desire,
and fulfill all your purpose."
Psalm 20:4

The psalm on page 50 was written by King David for people to pray for one another, that God would give them what they desire in their heart and bring about all that needs to happen in order to see His purpose for their lives come about. You can pray that for yourself, or have someone pray this over you. You can also pray it for someone else who needs encouragement.

God created you with special plans and purposes, He has great plans *for* you, and He has put gifts and talents *in* you. Ask God to help you recognize and appreciate the purpose He has for your life.

My Prayer to God

Dear Lord, I thank You that You have put special gifts, abilities, and talents in me that You will use for Your special purposes. Even though I don't see it all now, I know *You* do. I pray You will guide me in the way I should live so I never get off the path You have for me. Help me to appreciate everything I am able to do. Help me to excel in those things You want me to use for Your glory. I give myself to You. I ask that You would teach me to learn all the things I need to know. Help me to wait patiently for You to do good things in me. In Jesus' name I pray.

Other things I want to remember to pray about are…

_____

_____

_____

_____

_____

_____

_____

_____

_____

_____

6

How Should I Pray When I Feel Afraid?

Everyone is afraid of something. Kids today have a lot of fear, because there are many things to be afraid of. But God wants you to come to Him whenever you feel fearful and tell Him about it. That's because He wants to take away your fear. It's not that God doesn't know you are afraid. He does. But He wants to hear about it from *you*. He wants *you* to talk to *Him* and tell Him about why you are afraid.

God says to pray about everything. That seems like a lot of praying, doesn't it? But God cares about whatever *you* care about—even when it seems like what you care about is too enormous even for God. There is nothing too big or too small for you to pray about. And there is nothing too hard for Him. He is the God of the impossible. That means *He* can do what is impossible for us. He cares about the big things and the small things in your life.

You can be afraid of different things. Sometimes there are good reasons to be afraid. But often there is no reason to have fear.

We're just afraid that there *might* be. That's why you need to ask God to show you if there is a good reason when you feel afraid. For example, are you ever afraid when you are in the dark? It's true there are dangerous things that can happen in the dark, and because you can't see clearly, you might think these things will happen to you. But God can see *you* clearly in the dark. And when you ask Him to take away your fear, He will.

God is...

always greater than anything you fear.

Do you ever have bad dreams that stay with you after you wake up? Dreams are not real, but they can make you afraid. And your *fear* is *real,* even if what happened in your dream is *not real.* You can ask God to take that fear away. Do you sometimes feel afraid, but you don't know what you are afraid of exactly? You can have a *fear* of the *unknown.* That means you feel afraid because you don't know for sure what is out there. That's why so many kids are afraid of the dark. It's because they can't see what is there, if anything. If that happens to you, ask God to show you what is causing your fear and pray He will take your fear away. If your fear doesn't go away, ask your mom, dad, or another person you trust, to pray *with* you and *for* you about it. Don't ignore your feelings.

WHAT THE BIBLE SAYS

Jesus said,
"Where two or three are gathered together in My name,
I am there in the midst of them."
Matthew 18:20

That scripture means when you pray with even just *one other person* in Jesus' name, God is there *with* you in greater power. That means your *prayers* will have greater power. Knowing God's presence is with you will cause you to feel safer. It's also good to tell your mom or dad, or whoever takes care of you, about your fears. It's very powerful to pray with one or two people who love the Lord and know how powerful it is to pray to Him.

Remember...

No matter how big
the things you are afraid of seem,
God is far bigger than all of them,
and there is *nothing too hard* for *God*.

There is good fear and bad fear. Bad fear can make you sick and keep you stressed and upset, and it can keep you from doing things you need to do. *Good fear* is when you are afraid to do something you should *not* be doing. It can keep you from doing something that is *not good* to do. For example, if you are afraid to do something your mom or dad, or whoever takes care of you, told you *not* to do, then that is a *good* fear. *Good fear* can keep you from doing the *wrong thing*. *Bad fear* can keep you from doing the *right thing*.

What the Bible Says

"I sought the Lord, and He heard me,
and delivered me from all my fears."
Psalm 34:4

That means God hears you when you ask Him to take Your fears away, and He will set you free from them. If He doesn't take away your fear, ask God if the fear you have is a good fear, and if He is wanting to warn you about something. Good fear can prevent you from walking into a dangerous situation. Keep that in your mind.

God says that His love takes away all our fears. Every time you pray to God, you are getting closer to God, and He comes closer to you, and you are better able to feel His love for you.

What the Bible Says

"There is *no fear* in *love; but perfect love casts* out *fear*,
because fear involves torment.
But he who fears has not been made perfect in love."
1 John 4:18

That means if you want to get rid of fear, turn to God first. Only His love is perfect. And His love will take away your fear. You feel safe and unafraid when you sense His loving presence with you.

WHAT OTHER GIRLS SAY...

The things that girls fear most are:
"Something bad happening to my parents."
"Being kidnapped or killed by bad people."
"Being in a flood, fire, or earthquake."
"Being embarrassed in front of people."
"Not having any friends."
"Being around a bully or an angry person."
"Seeing a spider or snake close by."
"Giving a speech or report in front of people."
"Being in the dark."
"Not being liked by other people."
"Bad things happening in the world."

One of the best things you can do when you are afraid is to speak praise to God. Say, "Thank You, God, that You are here with me. Thank You that You are bigger than anything I am afraid of." Ask Him if there is really something to be afraid of right then, and call your mom or dad, or a family member, or whoever is taking care of you, to pray with you. They need to know whenever you are afraid so they can check to make sure if they need to do something to help you feel safer.

What makes you afraid? Write out your answer as a prayer. (For example, if you are afraid of the dark, write out a prayer that says, "Lord, I'm afraid of the dark. Help me to remember that You are always with me, even in the dark. Some other things I am afraid of are…")

_____

_____

_____

Don't ever forget that God is *always* on your side. He *always* wants to protect you from anything scary. So whenever you feel afraid, talk to Him immediately. He loves to hear from you.

My Prayer to God

Dear Lord, I pray You will take away all my fears. Help me to know if what I am afraid of is real or not real. Show me if I am afraid of something You don't want me to think about all the time. Teach me to understand when I have good fear that keeps me from doing something that is dangerous or wrong. Thank You for always being here for me when I call on You. I am grateful that You protect me because I seek You in my life, and I want to always live in a way that pleases You. When I feel afraid, remind me to praise You, because You are my all-powerful Father God and I am Your daughter. And when I praise You for all that You do, I can feel that You come closer to me. In Jesus' name I pray.

Other things I want to remember to pray about are…

_____

_____

_____

_____

_____

_____

_____

_____

_____

7

Will God Help Me Be Safe?

Yes, God can keep you safe. He promises to do that. But you must live His way and obey Him. So you need to ask Him to help you live *His* way. And you must always ask Him for *His protection* in everything you do.

You may be wondering, if God protects us, then why do bad things happen to good people? The truth is that God gives us all a free will. We can refuse to live God's way and go our own way instead. Or we can choose to follow God's way and ask Him to guide us and lead us. It's one thing to know who God is, but it's another to give your life to Him and ask Him to guide you every day. It's important to stay close to God by praying to Him, praising Him, obeying Him, and trusting in Him and His Word.

WHAT THE BIBLE SAYS

"Whoever trusts in the LORD shall be safe."
Proverbs 29:25

That means God will always help you to be safe. But you have to be following Him. If you are not following Him, you may choose to do something, or go someplace, that is not safe. You have to put your trust in God and let Him guide you.

Every day when you get up, say, "Thank You God for this new day. Lead me in everything I do today. I don't want to do just what I want to do. I want to do what You want. So help me to always know the right thing to do."

This is such an important prayer to pray because as you get older and become a teenager, you will have more and more opportunities to decide where you will go and when, and who you will go with. You will need to have a heart that is listening to God so He can guide you. That way He can always keep you safe.

WHAT THE BIBLE SAYS

"When you pass through the waters, *I will be with you*; and through the rivers, they shall not overflow you. When you walk through the fire, you shall not be burned, nor shall the flame scorch you."
Isaiah 43:2

That means whenever you feel unsafe or unsure for any reason, say, "Lord Jesus, protect me. Thank You that You are always with me. If there is something to be afraid of, show me. If not, help me to trust You to protect me and give me peace."

WHAT OTHER GIRLS SAY...

When some girls most often ask God to keep them safe:
"When I first get up."
"Whenever I need to go somewhere."
"Each time I walk anywhere."
"If I am in a car with anyone."
"Every night when I go to bed."
"Whenever I feel afraid."
"Every time I pray."

When do *you* most want to ask God to keep you safe?

_____

_____

_____

Remember...

You can't expect to always stay safe
if you are not obeying God,
and you must also obey the rules good people
give you in order to keep you safe.

WHAT THE BIBLE SAYS

"The LORD is my *rock* and my *fortress* and my *deliverer*;
my God, my *strength*, in whom I will trust;
my *shield* and the *horn* of my salvation, my *stronghold*.
I will call upon the LORD, who is worthy to be praised;
so shall I be saved from my enemies."
Psalm 18:2-3

A QUESTION FOR YOU

What are some of the rules your parents, teachers, or people who take care of you have given you to keep you safe?

_____

_____

_____

Read the following verses and write down some rules God shows you.

1. "Whatever we ask we receive from Him, because we keep His commandments and do those things that are pleasing in His sight" (1 John 3:22).

What do you need to do?

_____

_____

What happens when you do that?

_____

_____

2. "Because *you have made the LORD, who is my refuge, even the Most High, your dwelling place,* no evil shall befall you, nor shall any plague come near your dwelling" (Psalm 91:9-10).

What do you need to do?

_____

_____

What happens when you do that?

_____

_____

That means God will save you from any attack the enemy wants to bring on you. From these Bible verses, list what God wants to be to You. What are *you* supposed to do?

_____

_____

_____

There is something you need to know. You may already know

all about this. But if you don't know, you need to be made aware of it. And that is, there are evil people in the world. Very evil people. It's hard to imagine why anyone would choose to be this evil, but most evil people want money and power. And they will do whatever it takes to have more money and more power. God hates this evil, and He wants you to turn to Him every day and ask for His protection from it. He also wants you to do *your part* by staying close to Him and doing what He says to do.

Here are some great rules to remember so you can stay safe:

1. Don't ever get in a car with anyone you don't know.
2. Don't ever walk anywhere without looking around to see if it's safe.
3. Don't ever open the door of your house to someone you don't know.
4. Obey the people you trust who instruct you.
5. Check out the rules wherever you are.
6. Obey your parents or whoever takes care of you.
7. Don't be around anyone who makes you feel uncomfortable.
8. Tell someone you trust about anyone who scares you.
9. Don't talk to strangers on the internet or anywhere else.
10. If you hear a stranger talking to you on your computer, shut it off and tell a trusted adult immediately.

11. Don't ever try to meet a stranger you talk to on the internet.

12. Refuse to be influenced to do wrong by someone you think is a friend. If they do that, they are not a friend.

13. Don't let anyone touch you in a way that makes you feel uncomfortable—not even friends or family members. Tell someone you trust if that happens.

14. Don't go anyplace with anyone when you don't feel total peace about it.

WHAT THE BIBLE SAYS

"Your ears shall hear a word behind you, saying, 'This is the way, walk in it.'"
Isaiah 30:21

This means God will speak to your heart about what to do. *God will always guide you when you ask Him to.* But you need to talk to God every day, so you will become familiar with hearing Him speak to your heart. And that is how He will guide you. You will hear Him say, "Go *this* way and *not that* way."

My Prayer to God

Dear Father God, help me to always obey You. I know that if I do something wrong, I can come to You and confess it and repent of it—which means I have decided to never do it again—and You will forgive me. Teach me about Your ways and how You want me to live. Help me to obey my parents and teachers and the people who take care of me. Thank You that they look out for me so I won't get hurt. Help me to walk with You and talk to You every day, so I can learn to hear Your voice to my heart telling me what to do and guiding me where I should go and when. Make me always aware of what and who is around me. Give me the ability to sense when I am close to danger. Help me to trust You enough to always obey You. In Jesus' name I pray.

Other things I want to remember to pray about are…

_____

_____

_____

_____

_____

_____

_____

_____

8

Why Do I Need Discernment and How Do I Get It?

You may have already heard the word *discernment*. Many schools and churches are teaching their children about it. And the reason for that is because it's so needed for tweens and teens at this time. And the reason I know this is because the girls your age who I interviewed for this book brought it up to me. Some girls who have not heard the word *discernment* at all don't know what it is and why they need it, but it's a very important word to understand.

If you have discernment it means you have the ability to show good judgment and understanding in your personal life. You need to have discernment because it helps you to determine what is *true* about a person, place, or situation, and what isn't. That means you are able to judge or understand if something or someone is *good* or *not* good. Or if the place you are in is *safe* or *not* safe. And these days you absolutely must be able to discern those things.

One of God's greatest gifts to you is *wisdom.* Having wisdom means you are wise about situations and people, and you understand how to obey God. It's not just in your *brain.* God also gives you knowledge and understanding in your *spirit.* Like many of God's gifts, you have to ask Him for it. Every time you say, "Lord, please give me more wisdom," your wisdom will grow. Also, every time you read God's Word—the Bible—your wisdom grows.

WHAT THE BIBLE SAYS

"If any of you lacks wisdom, let him ask of God, who gives to all *liberally* and without *reproach,* and it will be given to him."
James 1:5

That means when you ask God for wisdom, He will help you to know what to do and what is right or wrong. *Liberally* means God will give you all the wisdom you need. And *without reproach* means He will never think you are asking for too much or asking too often.

You may be thinking, *Why do I need wisdom?* You need wisdom in order to always make wise decisions. And the wisdom God gives *you* is greater than the wisdom of those who don't know God. They have worldly wisdom. But you have *godly wisdom.* That means you can make a wise decision without even realizing you are doing it at the time because God has given you that gift.

WHAT THE BIBLE SAYS

"The LORD gives *wisdom*; from His mouth come *knowledge* and *understanding*; He stores up *sound wisdom* for the upright; He is a *shield* to those who walk uprightly; He *guards* the paths of justice, and *preserves* the way of His saints."
Proverbs 2:6-8

That means God will give you wisdom and understanding in order to *shield* you from danger. He will *guard* you and *keep* you safe. When you have godly wisdom, you will make the right decisions. The *upright* are people who always want to do the right thing and live God's way. The *saints* are people who know and love Jesus and who serve the Lord.

The most important thing about having the wisdom that *God* gives you is that you can have it in a moment's time right when you need it most. In an instant when you have to make a quick decision, you will make the right one because you have been praying and asking God all along to give you wisdom. It can protect you from harm.

WHAT THE BIBLE SAYS

"He shall give His angels charge over you,
to keep you in all your ways."
Psalm 91:11

That means not only will God keep you on the right path, and help you make *right decisions* and *good choices*, but He also sends the protection of angels to watch over you. (That seems to suggest that we have more than one angel.) But you must choose to live God's way and ask Him for more wisdom.

Remember...

God is always good, and it is God's enemy—
who is also *our* enemy—who comes to try and
do bad things. But you have power over your
enemy when you pray in Jesus' name.

"I will say of the LORD, 'He is my refuge and
my fortress, my *God, in whom I trust…*'
You will not fear the *terror* of night,
nor the *arrow* that flies by day,
nor the *pestilence* that stalks in the darkness."
Psalm 91:2,5-6 NIV

That means God will protect you day and night because you
have made Him your place of safety that you turn to every day.
And He will protect you from dangers you don't see coming.
Pestilence means a deadly disease that is spreading everywhere.
God will protect you from all that, but you still have to obey
God, and other people who are trying to help you.

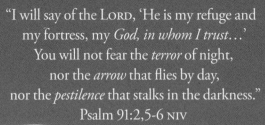

Remember…

When you have godly wisdom,
God will help you make the right decisions.
So turn to Him every day to ask for greater wisdom,
plus the ability to discern what you
personally need to know.

Discernment will help you recognize when a certain person makes you feel personally uncomfortable. If that happens, don't ignore it. Ask God to tell you, by the power of *His Spirit* speaking to *your spirit,* what to do. If you feel unsafe, or that something is wrong with the situation you're in, don't ignore that. Say, "Father God, show me everything I need to see about this person, this place, or this situation I am in." God will give a picture in your mind—or you will feel it in your heart—that speaks to you about what you need to do. For example, it is *not unwise* to have a friend. But it is *unwise* to have a friend who does not live a godly life. Even someone you think is a friend can do or say something that makes you feel uncomfortable. You need *personal discernment*—which is the ability to *discern* or *sense* something that *doesn't feel right to you.* It is something you personally feel, even if you don't know exactly why. Don't ignore those feelings. Ask God *why* you feel that way. Talk it over with your mom, dad, the person who takes care of you, or someone you totally trust, and ask them to pray with you about it.

Remember...

Never ignore what you sense
in your spirit about someone, some place,
or some situation; trust the discernment
God gives you.

Never trust a stranger or someone who could hurt you. Don't touch anyone who makes you feel uncomfortable. And don't let them touch you at all. You should also never be forced to *do* anything that makes you feel uncomfortable. When you have discernment, you will have a feeling or knowledge about who to trust and who not to. When you are with someone with whom you feel uncomfortable, get away from them as soon as you safely can.

WHAT OTHER GIRLS SAY...

What girls with discernment do when a situation, place, or person makes them feel uncomfortable:
"I leave the situation."
"I immediately get away from that person."
"I shut down the computer."
"I delete anything on my phone."
"I tell an adult I trust."
"I ask God for more discernment."
"I pray for God to protect me."
"I ask God to show me what to do."

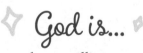

God is...

**always willing to
give you more wisdom and discernment
when you ask for it.**

If a person comes up to you that you don't know—or a person you do know but for some reason you don't feel safe around him or her—what should you do? (If you are not sure, ask your mom or dad, or a person who takes care of you, what they would want you to do.)

_____

_____

_____

Ask God to give you wisdom and discernment every day. There will never be a day when you don't need both so that you will always make good decisions. The reason it is so important for you to make the right decisions every day is that there is evil in the world, and evil people try to set traps for young girls. God wants you to have discernment from *Him* so you won't fall into any of those traps. Ask God to give you His wisdom and personal discernment for you so you can always make the right decisions for your life.

My Prayer to God

Dear Father God, I pray You will give me wisdom so I am always able to personally discern what the truth is about a person or a situation. Show me who to trust and who to avoid. Help me to quickly tell my parents, or an adult I trust, about anyone who makes me feel uneasy or uncomfortable. Teach me to trust the discernment You give me and never ignore it. Remind me to never talk to strangers, because I don't know what they might do. Show me clearly if there is someone who is a danger to me, or if I am ever in a dangerous situation or place. Give me discernment immediately if I am ever on a computer and I mistakenly come across a dangerous site. I trust that You will give me the discernment I need to stay safe. In Jesus' name I pray.

Other things I want to remember to pray about are…

_____

_____

_____

_____

_____

_____

_____

_____

_____

How Can I Always Have Good Relationships?

Every girl needs good relationships with friends and family. Both are important to your life. A relationship is how you and another person relate to each other. If your relationship is *enjoyable,* and you *both feel good* being around each other, and you *bring out the best* in each other, then that is a good relationship. You want *all* your *relationships* to be like that because they help your whole life to feel good. If you have a relationship with someone who often troubles you, or makes you feel sad, discouraged, uncomfortable, or bad about yourself—like you want to avoid that person, or you feel happier *not* being around them—then those are signs of a difficult or bad relationship.

Every girl likes to have good friends. She knows they are fun and valuable to her. But sometimes you can have a friend who doesn't turn out to be as good as you thought she was. If you have a friend who is difficult, pray for her and ask God what to do. Your prayers may help her to be a better friend. Or you may need to pray that each of you finds another friend who is more compatible.

What the Bible Says

"The righteous should choose his [her] friends carefully,
for the way of the wicked leads them astray."
Proverbs 12:26

That means *you choose* who you want to be your friends. So you must *choose carefully*. The way to do that is to ask God about who should be your friend. Pray about every possible friend who comes into your life. You can't *make* someone be your friend. That person has to *choose* to be *your* friend too.

We are often put together with people who wouldn't be our first choice for a friend, but we must try to make the best of it and be friendly to them. You definitely don't want to be a friend with someone who will lead you away from God, or cause you to do things that do not please God or your parents. After you get to know a person who could be a possible friend, ask God about whether she would be a good friend to you.

If you choose a person who does not turn out to be a good friend, you still have a choice to not be her friend anymore. Ask God to show you how to handle it. There is a way to do that so it doesn't hurt the person's feelings or make her angry. Ask your mom, dad, or best friend to help you.

The Bible says we become like our friends. If you spend time with a friend who has bad habits, you can end up being like them and develop the same bad habits. If you have a friend who is a bad influence on you, it can cause you to get in trouble. *Influence* means how one person can affect another. And a person can affect you in a good way or in a bad way. Pay attention to that.

A good friend, on the other hand, will bring out the best in you. She will influence you with good habits, and you can inspire good things in her as well.

WHAT OTHER GIRLS SAY...

Some girls want these qualities in a friend:
"She must love God and His ways."
"She must not do wrong or bad things."
"She must care about others."
"She must never act like a bully."
"She must always be kind."
"She must not say bad things about others."
"She must be easy to talk to."
"She must desire to always do what's right."

Pray for every friend you have throughout your life, and ask God to show you if you are good for each other. Ask Him if she is a good influence on you and if you are a good influence on her. Ask your mom and dad, or a close friend, if you are not sure. If you move to a new neighborhood or a new school, of course you will want to make new friends in that place. So pray as soon as you can that God will bring into your life new, godly friends. Keep praying about that until you find them—or *they* find *you*—and then pray for your friendships to always be pleasing to God. Always ask God to show you who would be a good friend to you.

God is...

the best friend you will ever have.

If you ever find yourself with a friend who does not bring out the best in you, or who is troubling to you, ask God to take that person out of your life. That doesn't mean she will disappear or something bad will happen to her. It means she will find another friend who would be better for her. Ask God to bless her with new friends or a new and better place to live. Or ask God to help her give her life to Him and learn to live *His* way.

Remember...

A friend who is a bad influence on you
will get you to do things that are against God's laws,
or talk you into doing something that
will get you into trouble.

You can have some friends who don't know God, because you may be the only one who tells them about God and shows them who He is. But your closest friends should be girls who love the Lord, because you will encourage each other in your walk with God.

A good friend is someone you can share your feelings with, and she won't judge you for them. She will pray with you about your problems, and talk with you about them, and help you see what you can do in order to make things better. And you can do the same for her. Every friendship can go through times where one of you gets mad or hurt, or you have disagreements, but with a *good friend* you can talk and pray together and work things out. That's because you both value each other and are willing to do that for a good friend.

WHAT THE BIBLE SAYS

"A friend loves at all times."
Proverbs 17:17

That means a good friend is always loving and kind. But liking or loving someone doesn't mean you never disagree with that person. And disagreeing with your friend does not mean you don't care about each other anymore. It doesn't mean either of you is a bad person. But if it happens all the time, it might mean you are not good for each other.

If a friend is always critical of you, or often says words that make you feel bad about yourself, that is not a good friend. If a friend always makes you feel sad after you have been with her, that is not a good friend—at least not for you. Ask God to bring you a new friend who is not critical and does not say things that cause you to feel bad.

Remember...

You don't choose your family members, but you *do choose* your friends. Ask God to help you choose wisely.

Praying for Your Family

One of the best ways to have good relationships with your family is to pray for each one of them. There is one thing you should keep in mind when you pray for any family member, and that is you can't *make* anyone else do what you think they should do—not even family members. You may be completely right in what you think they should do, but remember, God has given each of us free will. He lets us choose what we do or say. That's because He wants us to *choose* to *love Him* and *to live His way*. And He wants that for our family members too. And sometimes they can be the most difficult of all.

Friends may come and go, but your family will always be your family. That's why it's important to pray for them often. Your life will be so much happier if there isn't always anger, fighting, or distance between you and them. Pray for your relationships with your mother, father, brother, sister, grandmother, grandfather, aunts, uncles, cousins, stepmother, stepfather, or whoever takes care of you.

♪ A QUESTION FOR YOU ✓

Who are the family members you would most like to pray for?

_____

_____

_____

If you don't know what to pray for them—if it's not obvious—ask *them* how they would like you to pray for them. You can also ask God to show you how He would like you to pray for them. Write down what you want to pray for each person you mentioned above.

_____

_____

_____

Remember...

The more you pray,
the more answers to your prayers you will see.

WHAT OTHER GIRLS SAY...

How some girls like to pray for their family members:
"I pray for anything I know is bothering them."
"I pray for how I would like our relationship to be."
"I pray for what I would like God to do in our relationship."
"I pray for us to be kinder to one another."
"I pray we will talk more to one another."
"I pray that we can share how we feel with each other."
"I ask them what they want me to pray about for them."

WHAT THE BIBLE SAYS

"Honor your father and your mother, so that you may
live long in the land the LORD your God is giving you."
Exodus 20:12 NIV

That means you will live a long, good life if you honor your
mom and dad. One of the best ways to honor your father and

mother is to love and obey them. Another way to honor them is to pray for them.

One of the ways to pray for your mom and dad is that there will be great peace, unity, and love between them. *Unity* means that they agree on things without arguing.

Many kids don't have a mom or a dad living with them. There are many reasons for that. It could be because of divorce, or because someone died, or because someone left. I pray that none of those things ever happens to you, but if something like that has already happened, just know it's not your fault in any way. A mom or dad can make a decision that seriously affects the lives of their children, but that doesn't mean your life will be ruined. God can and will do great things in your life. You can grow up to be strong and smart and successful, and have a good relationship with God and others. God's plans for your life will happen no matter what any family member does or does not do.

WHAT OTHER GIRLS SAY...

Some of the ways girls like to honor their father and mother, or whoever takes care of them:
"I *tell* them I love them."
"I find ways to *show* my love to them."
"I *obey* them."
"I *do something* they will like."
"I *help* them do things."
"I *pray* for them."
"I *ask* them how they want me to pray for them."

What are some ways you can think of to honor your father or mother (or whoever takes care of you)?

_____

_____

_____

When you pray for your family, keep in mind that your prayers can be powerful in their lives and affect them in great ways. But they can still be determined to live in a way that doesn't seem right to you. If that happens, it doesn't mean you failed in some way or your prayers weren't powerful. It just means that they made a decision to do what *they* wanted to do.

Because good relationships are crucial to your happiness—and they always will be—praying for them is very important. Keep in mind, however, that not every relationship will be the way you want it to be. But don't get discouraged about that. Some people are difficult, and you can't change them. Thank God that He will always be a good friend to you, and He can bring good people into your life. And God never changes.

My Prayer to God

Dear Lord, please help me to always have good relationships with friends and family. Teach me how to find good, godly friends. Keep me away from friends who will not be a good influence on me. When a new friend comes into my life, help me to know whether she will be a good friend or not. Give me discernment to understand if we will be good friends for each other. Give me Your wisdom so that I will choose my friends wisely. Show me how to be a good friend to others. I also pray for my family relationships. I pray that my mom and dad will be kind to one another. If they are divorced, or either of them is not in the picture anymore, I pray that they will come to know You, Lord. Teach my mom and dad to pray together about things and not disagree. Give them Your peaceful Spirit, and cause them to always live in unity with other family members. Show me how to pray for all my family members so that we will all get along and love each other. In Jesus' name I pray.

Other things I want to remember to pray about are…

_____

_____

_____

_____

_____

10

What Simple Ways Can I Show Kindness to Others?

God plants seeds in your heart. And every time you pray—or read God's Word, or tell God how much you love Him, or praise and worship Him—He waters those seeds, just like you would water an apple tree. And just like an apple tree, fruit comes forth at the right time. God calls this *spiritual fruit* in your *heart* the "fruit of the Spirit."

WHAT THE BIBLE SAYS

"The fruit of the Spirit is love, joy, peace, *longsuffering*, kindness, goodness, faithfulness, gentleness, self-control. Against such there is no law."
Galatians 5:22-23

That means these seeds that come from God's Holy Spirit and are planted in you will grow. *Longsuffering* means having great patience. Who doesn't love and appreciate a person who is loving, joyful, peaceful, patient, kind, good, faithful, gentle, and able to always have self-control? We all need God's help to produce wonderful character traits like these.

I don't know if anyone is perfectly like all those things all the time. But God knows if you *want* to be able to see the fruit of the Spirit in you. Tell God that you want to have the fruit of His Spirit grow in you so it shows to others. God loves that prayer. He always answers it. That is the way to become a kind person—to invite *His* spirit of kindness to grow in you.

The fruit of the Spirit is what God plants in your heart when you first receive Jesus and become His daughter. Your heavenly Father plants these seeds of His Spirit in your heart, and His Holy Spirit causes them to grow. That happens more and more as you learn to talk to God, read His Word—which is His love letter to you—and choose to live His way. Ask God to grow these fruits up in you. This is not something you have to *force* yourself to *do.* It is something that develops in you when you walk with God every day and His Spirit is in you.

◆ WHAT OTHER GIRLS SAY... ◆

The ways girls like to show kindness to others:
"I think of what a particular person likes."
"I try to always be encouraging."
"I ask God to help me be forgiving."
"I ask God to show me what makes that person happy."
"I ask the person if there is anything I can do for her."
"I ask God to tell me any way a person might be struggling."
"I try to do small things that a person might appreciate."

Who are your two or three closest friends? What do you like most about each one?

_____

_____

_____

Make a list of your five closest family members. Write down a way you could show kindness to each one.

1. _____

2. _____

3. _____

4. _____

5. _____

What are some ways you would like others to show kindness to you?

_____

_____

_____

God is...

always kind.

God will plant seeds of kindness in you, and you can plant seeds of kindness in your relationships with others. It's amazing how quickly you can see the seeds of kindness you sow in your relationship grow into something great. The key is asking God about each family member and each friend that you want to do something kind for. Say, "What kind thing can I do for that person?" You don't have to do that for all of them every day. Just choose one at a time, and see what God shows you about what would bless that person.

Remember...

Every act of kindness and love you do
for another shows that person the love and
kindness of God. In that way you are a messenger
from God to them, because they experience
the heart of God through you.

I remember moving to a new city in a new state, and it seemed so different to me that I felt totally out of place. People there were not mean, but it was obvious I was not exactly like them, so I was ignored. But there was this one girl who I saw often because I went to where she worked to buy things I needed. She was always so kind to me, and I wanted to do something kind for her as a way of saying "I appreciate you, and I am here to help in any way I can." I asked God to show me how to bless her because I didn't know much about her, and He showed me something she needed. When I gave it to her, she was so grateful it surprised me. I would not have even thought of it if God had not brought it to my mind. That was years ago, and she has become one of my best friends. It was a seed of kindness God planted in my heart, and it grew into one of the best relationships in my life.

There might be a person in your life who is so difficult that the last thing you want to do is be kind to him or her. Actually, you may just want to avoid them. But sometimes that is not possible because your circumstances may have put you two together more often than you would like. In that situation, I have found the best way to handle your dreaded moment of being around them is to do *something kind* for them. It can be something simple.

If you don't know them really well, greet them with a smile and a "hi" and find something you admire in them and compliment them. I know it may be hard to do, but ask God to show you something good about that person. Is it her hair? Her nails? Her clothes? Her ability to do something? The way she helps people? The way she does her work? Whatever it is, when you are kind to her, you may see her change and become nicer. Ask her how she is doing and if she says, "Terrible," then ask if there is anything she wants you to pray about for her. Most people will say yes to being prayed for, even if they don't know the Lord. And your prayer will matter in that person's life. No matter if she says yes or no, tell her you will remember to pray for her when you are home.

There is one thing I should warn you about again, and that is there are evil people in the world. You are a beautiful young girl, and you are kind to people, so you might be more than a certain person can resist. You must have discernment about this. Ask God to show who you should not trust with your kindness. To a problem person, kindness can seem like an invitation into your life as if you are trying to get their attention. An evil person who has evil intentions is not someone you can do acts of kindness for because they cannot be trusted. This is going to be true for the rest of your life as a young woman who belongs to God.

So ask God to *give* you *discernment* about that. It is extremely important.

When you want to offer a simple act of kindness to a friend or family member, ask God to show you what you could *do* or *give* that would make that person happy. You may be surprised how much a simple gesture would please someone. That's because not enough people in the world will take the time or make the effort to do that. Or they don't feel they have anything to offer that someone would like. But *you* have the *love* of *God in you*. And everyone would appreciate some sign of His love offered to them through you.

My Prayer to God

Dear Lord, I pray that You would grow the fruit of the Spirit in me so that it clearly shows to others. Plant Your love, joy, and peace in my heart. Help me to show patience, kindness, and goodness to others. Teach me to be faithful, gentle, and self-controlled with others. In other words, make me to be like You. Show me how to always be a kind person. Give me the wisdom and discernment I need to understand if I am showing kindness to a person who is not nice and will take it the wrong way. I don't want to encourage that person to think they have an invitation into my life if they do not have my best interest in their heart. Show me ways to do good to others like I want them to do to me. In Jesus' name I pray.

Other things I want to remember to pray about are…

_____

_____

_____

_____

_____

_____

_____

_____

11

Can I Be Happy When I Don't Feel That Way?

To answer the question—Can I be happy when I don't feel that way?—the answer is *yes*! The reason you can do that is because even though your feelings can change in an instant, and the circumstances of your life can be changed in a moment as well, the good news is *God never changes*. He said in His Word, "I am the LORD, I do not change" (Malachi 3:6). And Jesus is always the same, so it means He never stops loving you.

That means everything you know about God will never change. You can trust Him on that. He is not going to stop loving you if you do something wrong. His love is *unconditional*. That means He *always loves* you. And He wants what is best for you. He knows that when you live *His* way—the way He says to live in His Word—your life is always going to be better. Remember, His laws and rules are for *your* benefit. It's the same with your mom or dad, or whoever takes care of you. They want a good life for you. They want you to be healthy and not sick, safe and not in danger, protected and not at risk of being hurt. That is exactly what God wants for you too.

God always *hears* and *answers* your prayers. *He* decides how He will answer your prayers and when. He may decide the answer is not yet, or no. When that happens, you have to remember that only *He* knows everything. No one else does. And you can trust that He always has your best interests in His heart.

Remember...

Look to God and praise Him,
even when things go wrong, because
He is always looking out for you.

The best way to start being happy when you don't feel happy is to talk to God. Tell Him all the things you love about Him. Thank Him for all the good things He has done for you. God loves to hear your words of appreciation to Him. That is called *praise*. You can praise Him for everything He has done for you. *Worship* is when we thank God for *who* He *is*. We worship God because He is the *King* of *kings* and our *heavenly Father*. We worship Him because He is greater than anything we face in our lives.

God is the King of the universe, yet He cares about the things you care about. He wants you to receive into your heart all the love, joy, and peace He has for you. These are things you can be happy about every day, no matter what.

When you thank God for loving you, and for all that He has given you, He will pour more of Himself into you—more of His love, peace, power, provision, protection, and blessings—just to name a few.

Remember...

Every time you feel sad,
thank God for everything you can think of
that you love about Him. Praise Him for all
He has done for you. Worship Him for who He is.
Whenever you do that, He will pour into you
His love, peace, and joy, and you will
feel happy that you know Him.

WHAT THE BIBLE SAYS

"In everything give thanks;
for this is the will of God
in Christ Jesus for you."
1 Thessalonians 5:18

That means every time you thank or praise God, you are doing God's will. So when you don't feel happy, thank and praise God for everything you can think of, no matter what your life feels like at the moment. It doesn't matter what the color of your eyes, hair, or skin is, or what the size or shape of your body is. You are beautiful. You are unique. And you have the beauty of the Lord in you. People see that. Thank God for who you are because every time you thank or praise Him, you are doing what pleases God most.

What are ten things you want to thank, praise, or worship God for?

1. _____
2. _____
3. _____
4. _____
5. _____
6. _____
7. _____
8. _____
9. _____
10. _____

Remember...

God's love and goodness never change,
and that is always a reason to praise Him—
even if life seems sad or bad.

Every time you speak thankful words to God and praise Him for what a wonderful and loving God He is, His presence will be with you in a more powerful way. And His presence always changes you and the way you feel. That's because in His presence things change. Even your circumstances can change.

WHAT THE BIBLE SAYS

"This people I have formed for Myself;
they shall declare My praise."
Isaiah 43:21

This means that God made you to praise Him. You were created to worship God, and that is your highest purpose. It is also true that you are to praise and worship Him no matter what is happening in your life—not just in good times, but in bad times as well.

If you remember that God is *always* worthy of your thanks, praise, and worship—and He is always greater than anything you face, or anything that is happening in your life—you can have a happy feeling inside you.

God is...
always with me.

If you feel unhappy, ask God if you have a good reason to feel that way. If you feel unhappy because something happened to your pet, or a close friend moved away, or a family member died, that is an understandable reason for feeling unhappy. Ask God to comfort you. However, if you feel unhappy because you are down on yourself, and you criticize yourself because you don't think you are good enough, that does not make God happy. Those words in your head are not from the Lord giving you advice. They are from the enemy, who comes to annoy all of us just because we belong to God. Don't let the enemy tell you lies to discourage you. Stop and thank God for *you* and *all you* can *do*. *Love* yourself, *respect* yourself, *stop criticizing* yourself, and give *thanks* for who God made *you* to *be*.

Do not compare yourself with anyone else. You are *you*, and that is always a *good thing*. Just concentrate on being the *best you* that you can be. You are not in competition with anyone else unless you choose to compete on a certain level, such as in a sport, or a music competition, or some other way. And that kind of competition is based on the skill of people, not a judgment on who you are and what your worth is as a person. You don't have to be in that specific competition unless you want to be. Don't look at other girls—such as friends, classmates, or family members—and measure yourself by them.

WHAT THE BIBLE SAYS

"Out of the abundance of the heart
the mouth speaks."
Matthew 12:34

That means your thoughts and words reflect what is in your heart. If you have been saying critical things about yourself—even to yourself—this doesn't reflect good thoughts and feelings about who God made you to be. That means the enemy of your soul, or a not-so-nice person, is trying to fill you with negative thoughts about you. Don't listen to those lies. Ask God to rescue you from them and turn your heart toward your heavenly Father. Remember, you are God's princess. You are special and beautifully created by God.

WHAT OTHER GIRLS SAY...

What some girls criticize about themselves:
"I don't like the way I look."
"I don't like the clothes I wear."
"I don't have good-enough skills."
"I don't feel accepted by others."
"I struggle with studying."
"I have a hard time focusing."
"I don't do anything well."

A QUESTION FOR YOU

What are some of the ways you are critical of yourself?

_____

_____

_____

Write out a prayer to God telling Him what you don't like about yourself. Ask Him to help you resist thinking those negative thoughts about you. Thank Him that He made you beautiful, gifted, accepted, loved, and smart, and that you have a high purpose.

_____

_____

_____

WHAT THE BIBLE SAYS

"I can do all things through Christ
who strengthens me."
Philippians 4:13

This means that when you feel weak or not good enough—or like you can't *be* or *do* enough—thank God that He is more than enough, and He can enable you to do all things that are His will for you to do. The way to handle that verse is to remember it. Memorize it. And say often to God, "Thank You that I can do all things through Jesus Christ who gives me His strength to do it."

The Bible says you can take your thoughts captive. You can refuse to listen to lies or damaging thoughts. If your thoughts are making you fearful, sad, angry, unhappy, or any other negative way, say this out loud, "Lord, help me to bring every thought I have under *my* control, and *Your* control, so I can always obey You" (2 Corinthians 10:5).

This is a very big issue for all young girls. The enemy—who is also God's enemy—will try to lure you with things that do not glorify God. He will start with negative thoughts about yourself. That is the first step to making you want to be like the world in the way you dress and act so you think you will be more accepted. But you are already accepted by God, and He has already given everything in order to make you His daughter forever. Because you are His, He will give you everything you need when you turn to Him.

WHAT THE BIBLE SAYS

Jesus said, "Whatever things you ask in prayer, believing, you will receive."
Matthew 21:22

Ask God to help you take your thoughts captive. Refuse to entertain thoughts that make you feel bad about yourself. God loves you so much, and He wants *you* to love *you* too. Love the you God made you to be. Love the things you *can* do, and don't be hard on yourself if you are still learning. Let God teach you in His way and His time. He has joy and happiness for you every day no matter what is happening in your life.

My Prayer to God

Dear Lord, thank You that You are good even when it seems like many things are going wrong in my life. Thank You that Your goodness and power are greater than anything that makes me feel unhappy. I give thanks and praise to You for all that You are in my life and everything You do for me. Thank You that You always pour Your love, peace, and joy into my heart when I come to You to tell you how I feel. Thank You that You always protect me, and Your love for me never fails. Help me to take control of my thoughts and not to criticize or say bad things about myself. Teach me to always speak words about myself that are the same as what You say about me. In Jesus' name I pray.

Other things I want to remember to pray about are…

_____

_____

_____

_____

_____

_____

_____

_____

_____

12

What Happens When I Read the Bible?

How would you like to read a book that can change you for the better every time you read even a few pages of it? It's a book that can affect the way you feel and the things you do in a positive way. And because God's Holy Spirit *dictated* this *book* to His trusted, faithful, and chosen believers over centuries of time, His Spirit is *in* it. That means when you read it, His Spirit speaks to your spirit and the words come alive in your heart. The Bible—God's Word—is the only book that can do that for you.

Don't be overwhelmed by how big it is. You don't have to read the whole Bible right now. You can just take one chapter and read through it. Or you can find a verse that especially speaks to *you,* and you can memorize it simply by saying that verse often. It will guide you so you won't get off the path God has for you.

What the Bible Says

"Your word is a *lamp* to my feet
and a *light* to my path."
Psalm 119:105

That means God's Word is always going to help you see where you're going. You won't feel like you're walking in the dark. You will be able to tell the difference between good and evil. Evil people can make themselves look good. But God gives you His light so you can see when something is not right or good in a person or situation. God shows you *how* to walk and *where* to walk because He lights up your path with His Word in your heart.

This also means that, sometimes when you feel like you can't see clearly, God will show you which decision to make, or what to do, or which way to go. Things will become clearer as you read God's Word because His Spirit speaks to your spirit as you connect with Him. You can ask God to reveal things to you that you want to know as you read. You may not even be reading specifically about what you want to know, but God will *speak* to your *heart*. You will feel like you know God better, and that is always a good thing.

Here are some more reasons to read God's Word—the Bible:

When you read God's Word, you are guided into the future God has for you. The Bible says, "Direct my steps by Your word" (Psalm 119:133). That means when you read the Bible, it helps you stay on the right path toward the great future God has for you. And you can't get there if you don't let Him guide you. Every time you read God's Word, you are better able to hear

Him speaking to your heart, leading you in the way He wants you to go.

When you read God's Word, you grow in wisdom. The Bible says, "The law of the LORD is perfect, converting the soul; the testimony of the LORD is sure, *making wise* the simple" (Psalm 19:7). That means God's Word is so *perfect*, it can *change* your *mind* if you are headed in the wrong direction. It's so *reliable* that it will make you a *wise person*. Every time you read God's Word, *wisdom grows* in you. Then you will have so much *discernment* that it will surprise you.

When you read the Bible, you learn how to obey God. The Bible says, "Give me understanding, and I shall keep Your law" (Psalm 119:34). If you don't *understand* what God's laws are, you can't *obey them*. The Bible *tells* you what His *laws* are, and God helps you obey them.

When you read God's Word, it helps you forgive others more quickly. The Bible says, "If you forgive men their trespasses, your heavenly Father will also forgive you" (Matthew 6:14). It can be very hard to forgive others sometimes, but when you read how many times forgiving is mentioned in the Bible, and how much Jesus forgave others, it softens your heart to forgive others so God will quickly forgive you.

When you read God's Word, you have greater peace. The Bible says, "Great peace have those who *love Your law*, and nothing causes them to stumble" (Psalm 119:165). You will be less likely to do things that will cause you to fall if you have God's Word in your heart every day.

When you read God's Word, your faith grows stronger. The Bible says, "Faith comes by *hearing*, and *hearing* by the *word* of *God*" (Romans 10:17). That means you can't grow in faith without reading and hearing the Word of God. When you read—or listen to the Bible being read—your *faith* gets *bigger*.

God is...

**always wanting to speak to your heart
from His Word—the Bible.**

WHAT OTHER GIRLS SAY...

Why some girls love to read God's Word:
"I want to know what's right and wrong."
"I want my mind to think clearer."
"I want to be a better person."
"I want to make good decisions."
"I want to do the right thing."
"I want to have bigger faith."
"I want to know God better."

How do you feel when you read God's Word? What happens in your heart when you read it or speak it?

_____

_____

_____

What is a favorite Bible verse you would like to memorize? If you can't think of one, choose one of the verses in any chapter in this book under "What the Bible Says." Or you can choose one of the three verses to remember below. Whatever verse you choose, write it down below. Then write it on another piece of paper so you can keep it where you will read it and say it every day. The more you say that verse over and over, the stronger it becomes in your mind and heart.

_____

_____

_____

Here are three verses you will always want to remember:

1. "Whatever things you *ask* in *prayer, believing,* you will *receive*" (Matthew 21:22).

2. "God has *not given* us a *spirit* of *fear,* but of *power* and of *love* and of a *sound mind*" (2 Timothy 1:7).

3. "I will never leave you nor forsake you" (Hebrews 13:5).

WHAT THE BIBLE SAYS

✦ "He who heeds the word wisely will find good,
and whoever trusts in the LORD, happy is he."
Proverbs 16:20

That means when you trust God and His Word, you will be much happier and experience good things.

Do you know that the more you hear God speaking to your heart in His Word, the more you can hear Him speaking to your heart when you are not actually reading His Word at that moment? That's because you are learning to better recognize God's voice speaking to your heart every time you read His Word. And that is a great thing. It's because when you are *in* the *world*, you will be able to *recognize* a *counterfeit* voice. When someone who is evil *pretends* to be a godly person, that person is a counterfeit.

Counterfeit money is printed on paper that someone made to look like real money, but it is worthless because it's actually fake. A counterfeit voice to your heart can come from the enemy pretending to be God. The enemy is always a counterfeit voice. When you read the Bible often, you will learn to hear God's voice so well that you will be able to identify the counterfeit voice of the enemy. If you heard the following words playing in your head saying, "You're not pretty," "You're not smart," "You don't have a purpose," or "No one likes you," would you think those are from *God* or from the enemy of your soul? Let me give you a hint. Those words would *never be from God*.

The Bible helps you learn about God and what He has done and what He promises to do. It also tells you what He wants to do *in you*. It tells you how much *God loves you*. It tells you how to think and live and pray in a way that pleases God. And that makes you happy! That's why the Bible will always be important to you.

My Prayer to God

Father God, I pray that You would help me to remember to read something in Your Word every day. Teach me to understand it—even if it is just one verse at a time. Give me a good memory so I can memorize verses well enough to be able to keep them in my heart and mind whenever I need to say them. I also need Your help to do what Your Word says to do. Your Word is living and powerful, and it comes alive in my heart every time I read it or speak it. I pray that You will do great things in me whenever I read or speak Your Word. In Jesus' name I pray.

Other things I want to remember to pray about are…

_____

_____

_____

_____

_____

_____

_____

_____

_____

_____

_____

13

Can I Really Make a Difference When I Pray?

I want to remind you to never forget that God loves children. When Jesus' disciples asked Him who was the greatest in the kingdom of God, He said, "Unless you change and become like little children, you will never enter the kingdom of heaven" (Matthew 18:3 NIV). Isn't that great news? I love that, don't you? That means you are very important to God. You are special. That's why God always hears your prayers. And He *wants* you to *talk* to *Him every day*.

When you understand how much God cares about *you,* and how much He wants to *hear* from *you,* it will *inspire* you to want to *talk* to *Him* often. And you will always have something you want to talk to God about or ask Him. Even though He knows what you need, He still wants to hear about it from you.

The more you come to your Father God to pray, the *bigger* your *faith* in God will grow, the more *powerful* your *prayers* will become, and the *more answers* to your prayers you will see. Remember that prayer is not telling God what to do. He knows what to do. But He wants to hear from *you* about *what you hope* in your *heart* He will do. Your prayers are important to Him, and even if you don't see the results of your prayers immediately, you can trust that your prayers are making a big difference.

WHAT OTHER GIRLS SAY...

What some girls feel about praying:
"It's very hard sometimes."
"It's fun because I can talk to God."
"It's about learning to trust that God is listening."
"It's difficult when I'm not sure how to pray about something."
"It's comforting when I tell God someone has hurt my feelings."
"It's knowing I must wait for the answers to come."
"It's challenging when the answer is not what I expected."

Remember...

Your prayers always make a difference.

Here are some things to remember about praying:
When you pray, it's *like throwing a small rock into a large, still*

body of water—like a pond or a lake. When the rock goes into the water, you can see ripples flow out from it in all directions. You may not see *every* ripple, or know where these ripples will end up, but you see something is changing.

When you pray, you don't see all the effects your prayers are having in the lives of people and situations you pray for—or even in your own life. But things are happening that you don't always see until later when you look back.

When you pray, it's like what happens in a football game, when the *quarterback* throws the *football* to someone on his team, who is supposed to *catch* the *ball* and *keep* running in the same direction the ball was flying. The person who catches the ball hopes to take it over the goal line for a touchdown. But if *someone* from the *opposing team* is able to reach up and catch the ball before it reaches the one who was supposed to catch it, that is called an *interception*. He intercepted the ball that was going one direction and then turns and runs the ball the *other way* and makes a *touchdown* for *his team.*

When you pray, you might see a situation or person that is perhaps headed in a direction that is not good. But you can reach up with your prayers and intercept what is headed one way and cause it to move in another direction. Even though you may not *see* what is happening as you pray, you can trust that *something powerful* is *happening.*

When you pray, you always make a difference, even though you may not see it at the time. And you don't have to worry that you might pray the wrong thing. God will never answer your prayer in a wrong way. God never makes a mistake.

Remember...

Your prayers have power because,
even when you feel powerless,
God is always more powerful than
anything you are concerned about.

I want to share with you something important you need to know if you want to always make a difference when you pray. And that is, your *praise* and *thanks* to God are *powerful*. The reason for that, it says in the Bible, is that *God dwells* in the *prayers* of His *people*.

WHAT THE BIBLE SAYS

David, one of the kings of Israel said to God,
"You are holy, enthroned in the praises of Israel."
Psalm 22:3

That means God's Spirit comes to live in our praise every time we praise Him. It's the closest we will ever be to God on earth. When it is our time to go and be with the Lord in heaven, we will still praise and worship Him. But then we will be *with*

Him, and it will be something we will want to do forever. We won't have to be reminded.

Our worship of God is the key to being close to Him because worship invites His presence to be close to us. Yes, God is everywhere, but the *power* of His *presence with us* is *felt* when we *worship* Him. Every time you worship and praise God, His presence comes to dwell more closely and powerfully in your life. And God doesn't just visit you for the moments you are praising Him. He walks more closely with you in your relationship with Him.

If you are ever afraid, or worried about something, or you are hurting in your heart because of something someone did or said, stop whatever you are doing and *thank God* for everything you can think of. *Praise* Him for what He has done for you in the past. *Worship* Him for who He is.

God is...

perfect love.

The best thing you can do every time you start to pray is to thank Him for all that He has done for you. (He has kept you safe.) Praise Him for all that He is to you. (He is your Protector.) And worship Him for who He is. (He is your heavenly Father, who loves you forever.)

For example, say something like this: "Thank You, Lord, for

helping me to do well on my test. I praise You for keeping me safe today. I worship You as my God of perfect love and peace."

🩵 A QUESTION FOR YOU 🩵

What things do you want to thank God for right now? (For example, "I want to thank God for my family and that He always provides for us.")

_____

_____

What things can you praise God for now? (For example, "Thank You, God, that You are always with me, and You will never leave me or forsake me.")

_____

_____

What is true about God that will always be a reason to worship Him? (For example, "Thank You, God, that You are the God of the impossible and there is nothing too hard for You.")

_____

_____

You can thank, praise, and worship God anytime you feel the need for more of God's love, peace, joy, and power in your life. And He will be there with you, blessing you with His presence, and helping you to pray powerful prayers that will make a *great difference* not only in *your* own *life*, but also in the *lives* of *other people* and *situations* you pray for.

Don't forget how one small stone, thrown in the water, can make many ripples; so one prayer can make many changes. And every time you pray, you are reaching up and intercepting a situation, or person, that may be heading in the wrong direction, but your prayer could be turning it around and heading it in the right direction.

When you pray, you can trust that God heard your prayers because you prayed in Jesus' name. And you prayed with a clean heart before God because you confessed to Him anything you have done, said, or thought that is wrong. And you asked God to forgive you. He always does and He always will, because you are His precious princess. And that's why you will always make a difference when you pray.

My Prayer to God

Dear Lord, thank You for teaching me how to pray. I praise You for loving me and caring about me. I worship You as my Father God, who is always with me. I want to always make a difference when I pray. So grow my faith to believe for the big things You will do. Thank You that You come closer to me every time I praise You for all that You do and worship You for who You are. I praise You for protecting me and my family. I worship You, Jesus, for saving me for Your kingdom so I can live with You forever. Thank You that I can make a difference when I pray because I am Your daughter. In Jesus' name I pray.

Other things I want to remember to pray about are…

_____

_____

_____

_____

_____

_____

_____

_____

_____

_____

14

How Do I Talk to People Who Don't Believe the Way I Do?

It can be difficult to know what to say when you talk with someone who doesn't believe like you do. You may not know exactly what they *do* believe, but you know—or you have heard—that they are not Christian. And you are not sure how they will react when they find out *you* are. I have found that the best thing to do in that situation is to *show* people who *you* are by being like Jesus. That means you are kind, thoughtful, accepting, loving, and respectful. Just like He is.

The more you know about who God is and what Jesus has done for you, the more at ease you will be. The more you understand about God's ways from His Word, the more it will become part of you, and the stronger a foundation you will be standing on.

How other girls feel about talking to people
who don't believe like they do:
"I feel awkward when I don't know what to say."
"I am worried I will say the wrong thing."
"I try to find something we have in common."
"I ask God to help me not say the wrong thing."
"I ask God to show me how to be kind and thoughtful."
"I pray that I can show God's love to them."

One of the nicest things you can do for people who believe in other gods, or in no god at all, is to ask them simple questions about their lives. Getting others to talk about themselves, and share what their life is like, is kind. It can give you an opportunity to ask them if you can pray for them about anything. You may be surprised at how many people will say yes. Don't pressure yourself about that. When you feel the Lord wants you to pray for someone, ask God and He will tell you what to do.

I am always surprised at how many people I don't know well will say yes when I ask them if I can pray for them—either right then or at a later time. I have had people who didn't believe in God at all, or they believed in another god—a false god—and they said yes when I asked if I could pray for them. If you ask a girl if she wants you to pray for her, and she says no, then just cheerfully say, "Okay." Then pray for her by yourself whenever God brings her to your mind. You don't have to become her best friend. Just letting her know that you see her and care about her can make a big difference in her life.

People who move into a new area from a very different place often feel they are invisible, and they desperately need someone to acknowledge them. It's a horrible feeling. I have had that experience myself when my mother moved so many times to a different town or state when I was a child. If someone even smiled or said "hi" to me, it made me feel like, "I *do* exist. Someone sees me. Maybe I can live through this."

Remember when you pray for someone else—anyone else—it's not your responsibility to make something happen or make the answer come true. That is God's work. *You* are the pray-er. *God* answers the prayer. Leave it in His hands.

I used to think, *What if I pray and the answer doesn't come—like it makes me look weak, as if my prayers aren't effective.* But our praying is about *God* and *not us.* So don't hesitate to pray for someone because you are worried God won't answer your prayer. The person you are praying for will be touched that you cared enough to pray for him or her. And you can tell the person you are praying for that your prayers don't mean they will always be answered immediately and in the exact way you prayed they would be. God decides. He will answer in the way He wants to and when the time is right. Praying for someone will always make that person feel loved. They will sense the love of God through your prayers. In fact, you may be the only picture of Jesus that person ever sees.

Your prayers for someone when they are not with you are also a good way to touch them. They will *feel* your prayers. God wants you to pray for others because your prayers not only affect the person you are praying for, but God also blesses you when you do that.

WHAT THE BIBLE SAYS

"Bear one another's burdens,
and so fulfill the law of Christ."
Galatians 6:2

That means when we pray for other people, we are helping to carry their *burden*—whatever that may be. Their *burden* is something they worry about or are concerned over, and for them it's like carrying something that is heavy on their shoulders or in their mind.

Ask God to give you words to say to anyone who doesn't believe like you. Ask Him to give you a love for that person you pray for, and He will. Your prayers are like seeds you plant that grow into something good if you keep feeding and watering them in prayer.

If you don't know what to pray for someone, just ask them. Say, "Is there anything on your mind or your heart that you would like me to pray about for you?" I know it can seem hard to pray for someone you don't know well, but the more you pray to God—just you and Him—the easier it will be for you to pray for others.

love.

Have you already experienced being around someone who believes differently than you do, and you didn't know what to say? What would you like to be able to communicate to that person? Write out a prayer below asking God to give you the words to say whenever you are in a situation like that. Write down anything He shows you.

_____

_____

_____

You should also remember that the stronger you are in your knowledge of God, and the more you understand how much your Father God loves you, the less chance you will be tempted into another religion or belief system. You won't want to betray or leave the heavenly Father you talk to every day. The more you think of God's promise to never leave or forsake *you*, the less likely you will ever leave or forsake *Him*. When you interact with people who don't believe the way you do, always be kind and respectful to them without being swayed by what they believe and do.

always on your side.

Remember...

All God asks you to do is
have His love in your heart for others.

Remember that whenever you feel weak—like you might feel when you are talking to someone who doesn't believe like you do—you can ask Jesus to strengthen you and give you words you need. He will do that.

My Prayer to God

Lord, I pray that You would show me how to talk to people who don't believe like I do or my family does, or who don't live like we do. Help me to be brave enough to ask people how they are and listen to what they say. Help me to discern if they are concerned about something. Give me courage to ask if I can pray for them. Give me great faith to believe that You always hear my prayer and will touch the person's heart for whom I am praying. Help me to communicate Your love for that person. Make me to be a *light* that shows *You* to *others*. Give me words to say that will help that person feel that they have value. In Jesus' name I pray.

Other things I want to remember to pray about are…

_____

_____

_____

_____

_____

_____

_____

_____

_____

_____

_____

15

What If My Prayer Is Not Answered?

We all have times when our prayers are not answered. It happens to everyone. That's because we always want more than God wants us to have at that moment. Or we ask for something that is not God's will for our life at that time. Even though God promises us He has more for us than we can even *think about* asking for, what He is talking about may be in the future. We often want the answer to our prayer to appear *now*.

WHAT THE BIBLE SAYS

"[God is] able to do
exceedingly *abundantly above all*
that we *ask* or *think*,
according to the *power* that works in *us*."
Ephesians 3:20

You must always keep in mind when waiting for the answer to prayer, that you don't have control over anyone else. *That means you can't pray for someone to do something you want him or her to do.* Because that person has a free will, they decide what they are going to do. You can pray that person will be *open* to what *God* wants them to do, and that they will *hear* from *God*, but that person decides what he or she will do.

Praying for your pets

One of the greatest losses you can have as a child is the death of your much-loved pet. It happens to everyone who has a pet, because pets don't live as long as people do. So if you have a pet, someday you will lose them. It's devastating. I remember every pet I and my children had that died. It was very sad, and it seemed like we would never get over it. However, you can start praying now that your pets will be protected. But just know they are not made to live forever, so one day they will be gone. Before that happens, ask God to comfort your broken heart, and thank Him that He chose *you* to be the one to take care of them.

Praying for people

We also don't have control over when people die. We can often be praying for a loved one to live and not die, and God will answer that prayer. But there will be a time when we are asking God to save the life of someone we love, and that person may die anyway. When that happens, you have to remember that *God* decides when it is time for a person to die. If the person you have been praying for knows Jesus, he or she will go to be with Him forever in peace, beauty, love, and perfect health. And you will see them again in heaven.

If you suffer the loss of a person you love, only God can walk you through it and eventually take away that pain. But you have to turn *to* God. Don't turn away from God because He didn't answer your prayer the way you wanted Him to. He is the one who will heal your hurting heart. Turn also to the people in your life who love you and understand the pain you feel. They and God will help you through it day by day. When you suffer any kind of loss, tell God how you are feeling every day, and ask Him to comfort you. He will do that.

WHAT THE BIBLE SAYS

"Blessed are those who mourn,
for they shall be comforted."
Matthew 5:4

That means if you ever lose someone and are mourning that loss, God will send His Holy Spirit to comfort you. Losing someone we love is a part of life because we all die. And I pray you do not ever have to go through that at your young age. But if you do, know that God will be with you through it. He will give you the special comfort you need to get through each day.

Don't worry if not all your prayers are answered. It may mean that your prayers have not been answered *yet*! The timing for what *you* want may not be *God's timing*. Or it could mean that God has something *better* for you than what you are wanting. Just keep praying and don't give up until you sense that it's okay to not pray anymore about that particular thing. Every time you pray, release your requests to God. And thank Him in advance for His answers to your prayers, whatever they may be.

WHAT THE BIBLE SAYS

"He gives power to the weak,
and to those who have no might
He increases strength."
Isaiah 40:29

That means God will give strength to you when you feel weak. When you don't get an answer to an important prayer, you can sometimes feel powerless—like you have no control over anything in your life. But you have to remember that you are young and God is still growing you up day by day. You may feel like nothing is moving in your life when you don't see the answers to your prayers. But when you walk with God, you are never standing still. You are always moving forward. God is always teaching you more about Himself because He wants you to trust Him more and more.

God's Word tells how God did so many miracles for His people, and yet they still complained against Him as if He had not done anything. They were rebellious against God. It says, "They *did not remember* His *power*" on the day He saved them from their enemy (Psalm 78:42). They saw God do powerful miracles in answer to their prayers, and yet they complained because He didn't do enough—He didn't do exactly what they wanted. That did not go over well with God. You must remember that God is always more powerful than anything you face. And He will take care of you because you love and trust Him.

♂ A QUESTION FOR YOU ♥

Have you prayed an important prayer that has not been answered? Or was your prayer not answered the way you wanted it to be? Write a prayer about that to God. For example, "Dear Lord, thank You that You always hear my prayers. But there is this prayer that has not been answered yet. Please help me to..."

_____

_____

_____

WHAT THE BIBLE SAYS

"Ask, and it will be given to you;
seek, and you will find;
knock, and it will be opened to you."
Luke 11:9

That means we must keep *asking* in prayer, keep *seeking* the Lord, and keep *knocking* at the door until God opens it for us.

God sometimes will answer your prayer right away, but often He takes longer than you want Him to. It's hard when you have to wait a long time. But you must keep praying no matter how long it takes. Sometimes your prayers *are* answered, but in a different way than you expected. Often you don't even recognize the answers to your prayers because God didn't answer them in the way you expected Him to.

Remember that God *always hears* your prayers, and He *will answer* you in *His way* and *His* time. So you can never be impatient with God for not answering in *your way* and *your time*. You have to trust Him and know He deeply loves you more than you can imagine, and you are important to Him. He always wants what is best for you, His precious daughter—His beautiful princess.

My Prayer to God

Lord, I thank You that You are always here for me no matter what happens. Even though my life changes, Your love for me never changes. If I ever lose a pet that has become like a close family member or friend to me, help me to get through the pain of that loss. If I experience the loss of a person I love, help me to get through it every day until the pain becomes less and less. I know that I can only make it through this loss if I stay close to You and You comfort me, as You said in Your Word You will do.

There is a prayer I have been praying for a while that has not been answered yet. Help me to know if I should keep on praying for that, or if I should put it in Your hands and let it go for a while. Teach me to have the patience to wait on You and not be discouraged if the answer is not what I expected. I love and trust You, Lord. In Jesus' name I pray.

Other things I want to remember to pray about are…

_____

_____

_____

_____

_____

_____

_____

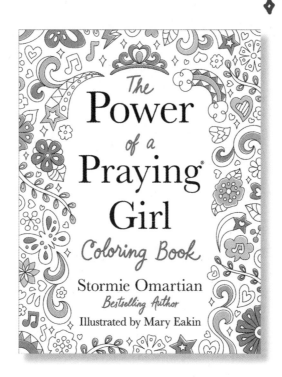

♥ Faith and Fun! ♥

Make colorful creations that reinforce what you have learned about prayer. Discover dozens of cool designs waiting for you to bring them to life with your crayons, markers, or colored pencils. These words and Scripture verses are perfect for tearing out and posting in your bedroom, in your locker, or on your refrigerator—wherever you'll look and be reminded to talk to God!

COMING IN MAY 2022